This Journal Belongs to:

____

Made in the USA
Las Vegas, NV
06 February 2022

43336751R00069